LIVING
UNDER THE
MASK

An Inspiring Story of
Turning Pain into Purpose

By Samantha Zayas

Edited by Lil Barcaski and Linda Hinkle

Published by: GWN Publishing

www.GWNPublishing.com

Cover Design: Kristina Conatser

ISBN: 978-1-959608-26-4

TABLE OF CONTENTS

Introduction 7

1: My Earliest Memories 11

2: The Brothers I Didn't Know I Had 17

3: Accepting Christ 23

4: Living Through My Mother's Depression 31

5: My Early Teens: Back into Foster Care 35

6: Back to Mom But Not For Long 43

7: A Better Life for Me and My Child 47

8: God Helps Me With a Difficult Decision 53

9: I Suffer with My Own Forms of Depression 57

10: No Good Deed Goes Unpunished 61

11: Big Moves and Changes 65

12: Failure is Not an Option. 69

13: My Husband and My Marriage Falls Apart 75

14: Overcoming Financial Difficulties. 79

15: Reconnecting With Someone Special: Triggers . . 85

16: Unexpected Struggles. 93

17: Big Building, Big Trauma, Big Work. 101

18: A Note on Permission. 109

19: Transparency is Key. 115

20: Living Your Best Life 129

Epilogue 133

Acknowledgments. 135

I dedicate this book to God, my children, friends, and family.

INTRODUCTION

I never understood why my life was so difficult, why my childhood was so incredibly hard until one day, I looked back at my life and had a moment of reflection. I saw where I was and took stock of the life I had created for myself and my children.

At that moment, I remembered these Bible verses.

—PROVERBS 3:5-6—

Trust in the Lord with all your heart and lean not on your own understanding; in all your ways submit to him, and he will make your paths straight.

—ROMANS 8:31, 37-39 NIV—

If God is for us, who can be against us? .... We are more than conquerors through him who loved us. For I am convinced that neither death nor life, neither angels nor demons, neither the present nor the future, nor any powers, neither height nor depth, nor anything else in all creation, will be able to separate us from the love of God that is in Christ Jesus our Lord.

—PSALM 59:1-4—

When Saul had sent men to watch David's house in order to kill him. Deliver me from my enemies, O God; protect me from those who rise up against me. Deliver me from evildoers and save me from bloodthirsty men. See how they lie in wait for me! Fierce men conspire against me for no offense or sin of mine, O LORD. I have done no wrong, yet they are ready to attack me. Arise to help me; look on my plight!

—PSALM 57:1—

Have mercy on me, O God, have mercy, for in You my soul takes refuge. I will take refuge in the shadow of Your wings until the danger has passed.

—JEREMIAH 1:5—

Before I formed you in the womb I knew you, and before you were born, I consecrated you; I appointed you a prophet to the nations.

—ISAIAH 40:29—

He gives strength to the weary and increases the power of the weak.

—PSALMS 147:3—

He heals the brokenhearted and binds up their wounds.

I began to realize that if I had not gone through all the pain and suffering, the battles and tribulations that I went through in life that left me with the scars and hurt I carry, I would not be the person I am today. You can't have a testimony without a test. If God had showed me what I had to go through in life to be where I am today, I would have turned back and told him, "No! I don't want that part or to go through that." I would not have known what I know today and be the person I am today. We all have our own testimony and story.

–CHAPTER 1–
MY EARLIEST MEMORIES

As a child, growing up in a dysfunctional home where everything felt lost and everything was a mess, I grew up feeling unloved, unwanted, and rejected. The only memories I had of growing up were so painful. I had a little girl in me crying for help my entire life. I just wanted to be noticed, loved, accepted, and wanted.

My life changed at the age of five years old when I was taken from my home and placed in a foster home. I was taken from my mother because of her physical abuse. At that point, my life was torn apart, and I was left in a dark place. All I remember is that I was in a strange place where everything was different, and I was abandoned to strangers. I remember being taken to one home for a few days and then moved to another home, and another. The cycle continued for months. During this period, there was never a time that I felt safe or secure.

In all of my memories of that period in my life, I was always sad and cried all day and every night, missing my mom. This went on for one whole year, the longest year of my life.

I was reunited with my mom after my year of being in the foster care system. As time went by, all I remember is that I never felt safe. There was always so much screaming, yelling, crying, and physical abuse, mental abuse, and verbal abuse; everything that created a place that was unsafe for a human being. Life continued, and all the bad memories continued to build. As the years passed, there never seemed to be a light at the end of the tunnel. I lived in a dark place and just wanted to escape.

I should explain that my mother suffers from bipolar disorder and severe depression disorder. Life was always a struggle having to deal with my mother being bipolar because her personality and mood changed constantly. I never knew what to expect. Things would change from one day to another or sometimes from second to second.

I know my mother had a hard life growing up, and she too saw many things a child should not have had to go through, but unfortunately, she never broke the cycle of physical, mental, and emotional abuse she herself had suffered in her childhood. She just continued on the same path taking it into her adult life and her version of motherhood.

I never understood why she had treated me so awfully, and I never felt the love or affection of the one person who should have been there for me growing up. I felt she hated me, and that I was a mistake because of all the awful words she would say to me.

My mother was very abusive to me as a child. She would beat me out of anger and the angrier she got, the worse the beatings were. There were a few times when she had beaten me so badly with a cane she took my arm out of the socket and left slashes on my back from the belt marks of her beatings. She would also choke me and lift me off the ground while I gasped for air.

She would say awful words to me such as, "I should have had an abortion with you. Why didn't I flush you down the toilet when I had the opportunity? I hate you, you're nobody, and will always be nobody."

As a child, I was forced to hear all the awful words that can come out of a human's mouth. My heart ached with pain, and I would cry, not understanding her and the things she did. I admit that I was no saint growing up. I talked back and refused to do chores, typical behavior of most children, I suppose, but I didn't understand how my mother could talk to me or treat me in such a way.

My self-esteem as a child was completely destroyed. All I wanted was someone to love me and care for me. As the years continued to pass by, my life became more challenging and harder.

I lived in a home with just my mom and my stepfather who I called dad. To me, this was the way a family was expected to be, a mom, dad, and children but we were far from the typical family unit.

My family was quite challenging. My stepfather, who raised me as his own, always treated me like his daughter. He showed me affection, and at times, I felt safe when he was around. He was the only person who said I love you. But there was a challenge. He had an addiction to drugs so, our life was even more difficult. He had no control over his addiction, and the addiction had complete control over him so, we all suffered emotionally.

When I was about four years old, we moved from New Jersey to Florida because my mom wanted to start a new life. I remember the three of us, leaving in a green car filled with clothes. When my mother met my stepfather, he was in a drug rehabilitation program called teen challenge. My mother fell in love quickly and married him. So, my mother wanted a new beginning for us, so she moved us to Florida in hopes that it would be a better place for all of us.

At the time, I did not know who my real father was, only the man who had raised me from four years old.

Even after the move to Florida, I remember that my mom was always crying. We had moved to a state where we had no family. Life got harder. My mom worked two jobs. I either stayed with friends or went to daycare while she worked.

Shortly after moving, my stepfather got with the wrong people and began using drugs again. I remember him taking me with him on drives, and we would end up at a house where he would leave me waiting in the car for long periods of time. We would eventually go home, and my mom would notice something was wrong with him and she would start arguing.

My father would walk away and hide in a room from the shame. I would go into the room and see him sitting on the floor crying and he would say to me, "Sam, I am trying to stop but I can't, and I don't know what to do." I would give him a hug while he sat crying and begged him to please stop. As a child, I also recall my mom going into drug houses to drag him out because she wanted him to change and save his life.

He would lie and steal for his addiction. He eventually ended up trying many rehabilitation programs but shortly after these attempts, he ended up in jail for stealing and doing other bad things. As a child, I saw so much, and to me it seemed all normal because it was the only life I knew.

REFLECTIONS: How does this chapter relate to things in your own life?

_____

_____

_____

_____

_____

_____

_____

_____

_____

_____

_____

_____

_____

_____

_____

_____

_____

_____

_____

_____

_____

_____

_____

–CHAPTER 2–
THE BROTHERS I DIDN'T KNOW I HAD

We later moved to an apartment and lived there for approximately one year. I was seven when I found out that I had two brothers from my mother's previous marriage. Apparently, that marriage was an unhealthy one as well from what I was told as a young child. My life was still very unstable and, of course, at my young age, I had no control. My brothers came to live with us when they were about 15 or 16 years old. This is when my life began to get even worse.

They hated me! My oldest brother was very angry and would often hit me. My oldest brother would cook and I often would refuse to eat what he made. Once, it angered him so much that he started screaming and threw a glass plate full of spaghetti at the wall. Then, he tied me up with duct tape and taped my mouth so I could not talk. He stood me in a corner because I had been screaming, and I told him I was going to tell my mom.

At the time, I didn't understand why my brothers were so angry. They both abused my mother physically and mentally. I mean truly physically abused her. They would come up to her and punch her in the face or drag her across the floor by her hair. My brothers would call her awful names like "bitch" and "fuck up". They would say things like, "suck my dick," "you're a worthless piece of shit," and many more horrible things.

My mother would cry. I was devastated at how my brothers treated her and I didn't understand what was happening and why they treated her so awfully. Unfortunately, it never stopped. In fact, it continued to happen until I moved out of my home at 16 and no longer had to witness the abuse.

By age nine, we had already moved four times and were getting ready to move again.

My mother ended up getting a divorce from my step father while he was in jail and then remarried. Her new husband mentally abused her the way my brothers did. Her new husband was also an alcoholic. I remember being grounded all the time and my mother ignoring me. I was having behavioral issues at home mainly because I was so angry at how horribly this man treated my mom and everything else that was happening with my brothers as well. I also was missing my stepfather who had raised me who was now in jail.

The marriage only lasted a few months.

My mom did not have many men in her life, but unfortunately, the ones she did allow in abused her. Growing up, there was always screaming, yelling, and breaking things and eventually, the police would arrive and arrest someone. Life as I knew it was just crazy all the time. I grew up so angry and so unhappy because all I wanted was a normal life.

Because of everything that had happened to me as a child growing up and all the awful things I had witnessed and withstood, I was very shy and reserved. This caused me to struggle with severe emotional issues.

Even in the mix of the madness, my favorite place to be was school. Even though I struggled academically because of everything that was happening in my home, school was still my safe place to escape. I had to work so hard for my grades, but with all that was happening, I never gave up.

My mother put me on medication because the doctors said I had ADHD. The side effects caused me to feel sleepy and drowsy. At the time, I couldn't understand what was happening. But school was my escape from the madness at home.

My mother continued to have lots of issues with my brothers. They would break walls and were constantly physically abusive towards her. They had so much anger. After about a year of being in the new home, we were moving again. While getting ready to move, my stepfather was released from jail, and my mother and he reunited.

During all these years, my mother's symptoms from her depression and bipolar disorder seemed to get worse. At the time, I had no idea my mother was bipolar because it wasn't until I was about 10 or 11 years old when I found out she had this diagnosis. My whole life I just thought her behavior was normal in the way she treated me.

I was always jealous of my friends because they all seemed to have what I thought was a perfect life. I hated my life, and everything about it.

At roughly age 11 or 12, my life changed again for the worse. My oldest brother began touching my private areas inappropriately, and this happened more than once. Who would ever think a loved one could do this to a child?

My brother had an addiction to drugs and alcohol. Life got harder for me. When I tried to move away from him, he would squeeze my arm. I was already so scared of him from all the physical harm he had done to me and my mother that I would just stay still and pray to God for him to stop. I always remember he would have a bottle of beer in his hand. I even remember the name of the beer. It was called Old

English. I always felt disgusted to be near him and so unsafe. I would just go to my room and cry for hours.

I grew up with this hurt for many years. I became rebellious and angry, and I hated everyone. My whole world was upside down.

REFLECTIONS: How does this chapter relate to things in your own life?

–CHAPTER 3–
ACCEPTING CHRIST

We continued to deal with my stepfather doing drugs and my brothers in and out of jail or doing drugs and dealing with their chaos.

Life really sucked. Due to my mother's depression, I had to grow up fast. I had to learn to cook, clean, and take care of the home. She would at times forget to pay the bills, and I had to remind her. She slept a lot and was always crying.

My mother also tried to commit suicide many times. On one occasion, I walked into her bathroom to find that she had slit her wrist and was sitting on the floor bleeding. She looked at me and told me that if she ever died or killed herself that it would be my fault. I burst into tears begging her to please stop saying these things. I was so scared and remember praying to God to please never let her die or kill herself because I would live with the guilt for the rest of my life.

Then, there was another time I went to check on her in her room, and she had taken all her prescription medication at once and was unconscious. I quickly called 911 and cried by her bedside praying to God to please not take my mom. The ambulance arrived and found her unconscious and saw a suicide letter she had written. My mother was quickly transported to the hospital and shortly after was Baker-acted and placed in a psych ward for a few days.

One Friday night, a friend from school invited me to their church for youth night. I sat there crying endless hot tears, running down my face during the praise and worship. I fell to my knees and cried to God asking him to please change my life. I felt that I would do anything to have the chance at a different life.

During praise and worship, the lights were very dim, and the church was dark. The only lights were the ones on the altar. In that darkness, they called people up for prayer proclaiming that the people who wanted to accept Jesus Christ as their Lord and Savior would be rewarded and that their life would change for the better. So, I stood up and went to the altar.

There were so many people. I repeated the words the preacher said, "Dear God, I want to be a part of your family. You said in Your Word, that if I acknowledge that You raised Jesus from the dead, and that I accept Him as my Lord and Savior, I would be saved. So God, I now say that I believe You raised Jesus from the dead and that He is alive and well. I accept Him as my personal Lord and Savior. I believe I am a sinner, and

I ask for your forgiveness. Thank you, Father God, for forgiving me, saving me, and giving me eternal life."

—JOHN 3:16—

For God so loved the world, that he gave his only begotten Son, that whosoever believeth in him should not perish, but have everlasting life."

—ROMANS 10:13—

Whosoever calls on the name of the Lord shall be saved.

"Whosoever" means you!

Right afterwards, I felt so different. I felt so relieved, and after that, I just kept going to church with my friends. I even remember inviting my mom to church. I became very interested in studying the Bible.

The Jehovah's Witnesses would come knock on our door every Saturday. One day, I opened the door and stopped to listen to what they had to say. I got even more interested and asked if they could come back and teach me about the Bible. When they would come, I would sit outside on a chair and listen to them, and they would teach me all about the Bible and break down the meanings of each passage when I didn't understand them.

I met a friend who was a Jehovah's Witness, and she invited me to her church. Church then became an escape place for me to go once or twice a week. At the time, I really liked their church because they explained the Bible in its entirety as opposed to when I went to other churches where the preacher or people would not do so in such detail.

Then I began to study the Mormon religion but was not as interested in that as I was already in the Jehovah's Witness and Christian churches. Reading the Bible and having someone explain it to me gave me hope, and all I knew was to hold onto my hope and believe in God's words which said that everything was going to be okay.

I was so excited to go to church school every Sunday. The bus would come by and pick me up to take me to a Baptist church for Sunday school. I would go alone while my mom was home sleeping. When I came home, I would be so excited, longing to tell my mom everything I had learned. They even gave me my first Bible. Even though things were so crazy at home, both school and church became my escape from all the madness.

Eventually, I got my mom to go to church. We would go every Sunday to a Spanish church. But the teachings at that church did not sit well with me, and

I really did not understand the way they explained the Bible. I would go just to accompany my mother. I saw so many things happening in the church that were wrong.

My mom would cry at church and ask for forgiveness, but when we got home she would go right back to fighting, cursing, and yelling. Her behavior did not get better; at church she was one way and at home another. It was as if she was living a double life. She didn't want people, especially at church, to see her for who she really was. I never really understood why.

I went to a private Christian school for about two years on a scholarship program for my ADHD so I could be in smaller classes. But once I got to middle school, I asked my mom to put me in a regular school. I no longer wanted to go to a church school. I began to distance myself from God because I was angry and disappointed that nothing at home was changing.

My mother would say this scripture to me over and over.

—EXODUS 20:12—

Honor thy father and thy mother: that thy days may be long upon the land which the Lord thy God giveth thee.

She would say that talking back to her was not honoring her and that God was going to punish me for my bad behavior.

I would talk to God and tell him, "I am trying to honor my mom but she's so mean to me. How can I love her and be nice to her when she treats me so meanly? Why does she hate me? Why didn't you give me to another family?"

REFLECTIONS: How does this chapter
relate to things in your own life?

_____

_____

_____

_____

_____

_____

_____

_____

_____

_____

_____

_____

_____

_____

_____

_____

_____

_____

_____

_____

_____

_____

_____

_____

_____

_____

_____

_____

_____

−CHAPTER 4−
LIVING THROUGH MY MOTHER'S DEPRESSION

*M*y mother would emotionally and mentally manipulate me so much, it was very hurtful. The memories got worse as the years passed. We never celebrated the holidays because my mother was so depressed and didn't want to do anything. One Thanksgiving, my mother was so angry and upset, she broke all the dishes in the house.

I hated the holidays. I hated Christmas the most. One year, my mom took me to Walmart to get a few Christmas gifts. I wrapped them and put them under the tree for myself waiting to open them for Christmas. Yes, I knew what they were, but I just wanted to feel surprised like all children want on Christmas. I just wanted to experience that kind of excitement for once. I did not have an imagination. I didn't even believe in Santa Claus or any of those childhood beliefs.

On another terrible Christmas Day, my mother had a huge argument with my brothers. She came tearing out of her room, grabbed the Christmas tree, and threw it across the floor. All the Christmas ornaments broke and there were shards of broken painted glass from the ornaments and pine needles everywhere. The holidays were the worst part of the year for me. While all my friends were spending time with their family, I was just sitting in a room crying my eyes out.

On vacation breaks from school, I would visit my grandmother in New Jersey for a few days. At age nine, I finally met my biological father who also lived in New Jersey. About two years later, I met him for the second time but by then he was in prison. My life growing up was just such a mess. I was embarrassed and ashamed of the family I had. I also remember us not being around family and my mother not having any family gatherings or us being invited anywhere due to my mother's instability and her dysfunction. I didn't really know my mother's side of her family at all.

I can't really remember happy times or pleasant memories related to growing up. My mom and I would argue about everything. She was constantly depressed and broke every promise she ever made to me. For example, she told me we were going to Disney World, to the movies, and many other places. Unfortunately, due to her depression, she could not function causing her to break every promise.

I remember like these promises like they were made yesterday. I was so sad and discouraged. She promised so much and would always leave me hanging, always waiting, yet nothing she promised ever happened.

When I was 13 years old, my mother called the police and had me taken to the juvenile detention center. I was having a hard time in my teenage years and was angry and rebellious. She lied about the extent of things that I did, and they left me in the detention center for two weeks. My heart was shattered. I no longer wanted to live and to tried to kill myself on multiple occasions. I hated my life and wanted it to end. I told the guard that I wanted to kill myself and, of course, they immediately sent me to the hospital and put me in a mental institution for a three-day evaluation. The day I was released to go home, my mother was driving us back to the house, and I opened the car door while it was still moving and jumped out the door. I just wanted all the pain and misery to end. But she just stopped the car, forced me back into it, and took me back to the hell we were living in.

REFLECTIONS: How does this chapter relate to things in your own life?

—CHAPTER 5—
MY EARLY TEENS: BACK INTO FOSTER CARE

My life got worse. My mother got a call that my stepfather was found in an abandoned house and was unconscious. I recall my mom and I driving to this place.

When we walked in the door, we found my stepfather laying on the floor naked with a blanket covering him up. My reaction and thoughts were that he was dying right in front of me. His skin color was changing and the enamel of his teeth was coming off. I cried so much. The pain was so real it felt like my heart was caving in, and I didn't know what to do.

My mom quickly called 911. When the ambulance arrived, they put him on a board to transport him to the hospital. We followed the paramedics out of the abandoned house and began driving behind the ambulance. All of a sudden, the ambulance stopped in the middle of the road due to my stepfather going into cardiac arrest, and they had to resuscitate him.

When we arrived at the hospital, he was examined and the doctor came out to the waiting area and told my mom and me that there was no hope and that she needed to go prepare for his funeral.

My father was in a coma for over 30 days. We would visit him daily. After a long journey, God had given him a second chance at life. Once he was released, he was sent to rehab to relearn basic life skills. After a few months in rehab, he was released. He then decided he wanted to start his own life. So, he moved into his own place.

When I reached my teen years. I had tried to call Child Protective Services (CPS) on many occasions and made complaints about my mother at school to my guidance counselor, but when CPS would come to our home, they would never find anything wrong. My mom would lie and tell them that I was a teenager who was acting rebellious and just wanted to do whatever I wanted.

I ran away from home on multiple occasions. And when I did try to stay, my mom would get angry and kick me out of the house because of a disagreement. One night, my mother kicked me out of the house, and the closest place for me to sleep was at a nearby playground across from our house. I would watch my house and wait for her to go to sleep so I could sneak in and get my clothes to go to school. Even through all the madness and disappointment, I continued to go to the one place I felt safe, which was school.

At 14 years old, I simply gave up because of everything that was going on. I had tried everything to make things work but I no longer wanted to live with my family. The final episode leading me back into foster care was when my mother had a nervous breakdown causing her to lose control and break everything in the house. She shattered the glass tabletop and all the dishware and many other items. There was glass absolutely everywhere, and I got injured from the flying glass. I was petrified.

This was the worst she had ever been. I had not seen my mother in quite this horrible of a state of mind before. So, I called 911, and the police arrived and saw all the broken glass and the disarray of our home. My mother ended up getting arrested for child abuse and neglect and was once again Baker-acted. They put her in a facility for her behavior at first but ultimately she was taken to jail.

That was when I was finally taken back into foster care. At first, foolishly, I thought life was going to be better, but I was mistaken. I was embarrassed, ashamed, angry and just wanted it to all end!! There were so many nights when I wanted to take my life because I couldn't take the pain any more. I hated my life. I had no one to turn to or to help me. I had no control over anything. But I continued going to school. Somehow, I was on a mission. I was determined to graduate and become someone and prove that I could be different.

I was given months of individual counseling and family counseling with my mom to try to help us reunify. It was during those sessions that I was finally able to tell my mother the truth of what my oldest brother had done to me. She became angry and accused me of lying. When she said she did not believe me, I was furious and told her I was done with her. I hated her. I was telling her the truth. How could she be this awful?

While I was in foster care, my stepfather finally passed away. He was once again doing drugs and it caused him to have heart failure.

I was so angry, I started fighting and getting into trouble. I ran anyway from foster care a few times because I hated the homes I was placed in. One day, I told my foster parents I was going to the library to study but I lied. Instead, I had a friend's mother take me to the airport. My grandmother had purchased a ticket for me to fly to New Jersey. I wanted to be with my family. My aunts, my mother's sisters, picked me up from the Atlantic City airport.

While in Camden, New Jersey, my family put me in different places to hide me so the State of Florida would not find me. One day, a family member took me to a friend's house so I could stay where no one would suspect I would be. It was in an apartment building near a highway and there was a liquor store across the street. The apartment was so dirty. The lady I was placed with was living with her children, but had a room for me to reside in while I stayed with them. I had to clean and cook for everyone.

One night I went into the kitchen to eat. and there were mice all over the kitchen. I started screaming. The mice scared me. I had never seen a mouse before. I was petrified and hungry, but I could not eat. The lady quickly came out of her room and started laughing at me. She said, "Girl, you act like you have never seen a mouse before."

I replied "No! I have never seen a mouse before." There were mice everywhere, in the oven, in the boxes of cereal in the pantry, and in the cabinets. I just could not take any more, so I ran back into my room.

After being there for a few days, the lady decided to make fun of me because I was scared of the mice. She began to throw the mice in the room where I was sleeping. She thought it was funny to throw them on my bed. I would run around the room screaming, and the mice would run from one side of the room to the other. I was going in circles from fear. I sat on the corner of the bed crying because I was so scared, and I wanted to leave but I didn't know where to go and was not even sure where I was. I stopped eating and was not sleeping. I would just cry for hours in the room.

One day, I was looking out the window and saw my uncle standing outside. I started banging on the window and screaming. He looked up and saw me. I begged him to please come get me.

My uncle knocked on the door, and the lady let him in. He took me out of that house with the little bit of clothes I had and took me to live at a family member's house for a few days.

While in New Jersey, I tried to enroll back into school but my uncle moved me to yet another family member's house until eventually I was caught by the state. Someone from New Jersey told my mom where I was staying. She called the police and told them where to find me, and I was returned to Florida.

—EPHESIANS 6:4—

"Fathers do not provoke your children to anger by the way you treat them. Rather, bring them up with the discipline and instruction that comes from the Lord."

REFLECTIONS: How does this chapter
relate to things in your own life?

—CHAPTER 6—
BACK TO MOM BUT NOT FOR LONG

At this point, I was 15 and was forced to be sent home to my mother. The day I got back, we went to meet with my oldest brother. My mother and I got into an argument in the car, and I remember my brother coming to the car yelling at me. I said some awful words because I was angry to be back in the same old mess. He pulled me out of the car, and I started running. He chased me down the main street and when he finally caught up to me, he dragged me by my hair up the street. I cried and cried. I hated him with everything in me. And my mother did nothing to help me.

After being sent back home, I was determined to graduate high school. I graduated at 16 years old and moved to New Jersey where I enrolled in a nursing program. While living in New Jersey, I worked at McDonalds and still attended school. At this point, I was 17 and already had my own apartment.

By this time, I was getting out into the real world, and I started to meet people and make friends. It was not long before I met the man who became my daughter's father. He had his own place and seemed as though he was pretty put together, but little did I know what I was getting myself into.

I guess I was looking for love in the wrong places. He started to abuse me not very long after getting into the relationship. He would hit me when he was angry and blame me for upsetting him. He broke my car windows and hid my car keys so I could not leave the house. He would lie to me about everything and cheat on me, even sleeping with other women. He would stalk me and would follow me if I stayed away.

Of course, after doing something heinous or inappropriate, he would cry and beg me to return saying that he was sorry and promising that he was going to change. I did not know how to escape and was scared to tell anyone so I would walk around like everything was okay. He would force me to have sex with him and I would cry and hope he would stop.

I ended up getting pregnant with my first child. Despite me being pregnant, the relationship was completely toxic, and the physical and mental abuse continued. I was scared all the time and wanted to get out but had no support and was afraid to tell anyone. I felt like I had nowhere to go so I decided to move back to Florida because it was all I knew.

After completing the nursing program, I moved away but my boyfriend wouldn't let me leave without him, so he went with me. We took a Greyhound bus that took us two days to travel to get to Florida. Prior to getting there, we had stayed in a motel for a week waiting for me to receive my student loan money so I could have enough money to pay for the trip and have money for a room for rent when we arrived in Florida. I had secured a room and had done the necessary paperwork to have somewhere to live when we arrived.

Things escalated and got worse once we got to Florida. Even while pregnant, I worked to support him and myself. I enrolled back into college when I got to Florida and found a job at Wendy's working full time while going to college part-time. This man, who was going to be the father of my child, was 26 years old at the time and I was still only 17. He was very manipulative, controlling, violent, and abusive in so many ways. He would stalk me at the college to see if anyone was talking to me or showing me any kind of attention. Eventually, he would not allow me to go to school at all. He would drive me to work and back to the place we were staying and watched my every move.

One day during my pregnancy, when I was about five months along, he became angry during an argument and he choked and hit me.

REFLECTIONS: How does this chapter relate to things in your own life?

CHAPTER 7

A BETTER LIFE FOR ME AND MY CHILD

I had had enough of all the abuse. I finally had the courage to ask for help. I had no choice but to call my mom and ask her for help. I ended up calling the police, and my child's father was arrested. This was the end of the abusive relationship. I reenrolled in school to continue my education while pregnant. I always wanted a better life and future for myself and now for the child I was going to be bringing into the world.

During the last month of my pregnancy, my mother was surprisingly very kind to me. She took care of me and made sure I had everything for myself and my daughter. After having my daughter, my whole life changed. She was the most beautiful baby my eyes had ever seen. While laying with my daughter in the hospital, I promised myself that I was going to love her unconditionally and give her the life I never had. I also promised her and myself that I would never allow anyone to harm her. My focus and priority became to provide her a safe, secure, and stable life.

—I CORINTHIANS 13:4-7—

Love is patient, love is kind. It does not envy, it does not boast, it is not proud. It does not dishonor others, it is not self-seeking, it is not easily angered, it keeps no record of wrongs. Love does not delight in evil but rejoices with the truth. It always protects, always trusts, always hopes, always perseveres.

My mother was present during my labor, and when I was released from the hospital, we went home, and our relationship seemed great. I was having to deal with the court for my daughter's father by taking domestic violence classes and parenting classes.

The great relationship with my mother did not last very long. After a few months, my mother started arguing and wanted me out of her house due to a disagreement of opinion on how to raise my daughter. I remember like it was yesterday. She came out of the house screaming and broke my car windshield with a black jack while the baby was in the back seat in her car seat because I had told her I found a place and I was moving out.

I immediately had a flashback of all the abuse I had gone through growing up. I was determined my daughter was not going to go through the same issues I went through. If you recall, in the beginning of my story, I said my mother was bipolar. In this episode, her personality had changed, and she had blacked out, out of anger. When I saw her reaction, I was done. I left the car where it was and walked to a friend's house with my daughter.

After a few days, the car was fixed, so I left. While I was waiting for the apartment to be ready, for a few days, my daughter and I slept in my car. I had no money for a hotel or any place to go. The only money I had was the security deposit and first month's rent. Once I left my mother's house for the last time, I was determined I would never go back home.

What kept me going was remembering what I was taught from Bible school.

—JOHN 3:16—

God so loved the world that he gave his only Son, so that everyone who believes in him won't perish but will have eternal life.

—ROMANS 8:28—

We know that God works all things together for good for the ones who love God, for those who are called according to his purpose.

At one point in my life, after having my daughter, I had to live off government assistance SNAP, TANF, and WIC. I was so embarrassed and ashamed because growing up I saw my mother, while working, still living off government assistance and she could not progress in life because if she made a dollar more, all her benefits would have been taken away from her. We lived below poverty-level income.

When I moved away, I struggled and I always remembered the Bible verses.

—JOHN 10:10—

The thief cometh not, but for to steal, and to kill, and to destroy. I am come that they might have life, and that they might have it more abundantly.

—PSALM 23:1-6—

The Lord is my shepherd; I shall not want.

He maketh me to lie down in green pastures: he leadeth me beside the still waters.

He restoreth my soul: he leadeth me in the paths of righteousness for his name's sake.

Yea, though I walk through the valley of the shadow of death, I will fear no evil: for thou art with me; thy rod and thy staff they comfort me.

Thou preparest a table before me in the presence of mine enemies: thou anointest my head with oil; my cup runneth over.

Surely goodness and mercy shall follow me all the days of my life: and I will dwell in the house of the Lord forever.

REFLECTIONS: How does this chapter relate to things in your own life?

−CHAPTER 8−
GOD HELPS ME WITH A DIFFICULT DECISION

I was working two jobs and going to school but always remembered the promises God had given me. I continued to work, and my daughter went to a friend's house so I could go to school two days a week and continue working both jobs to survive and provide a safe home. It was hard, but I was determined to break the cycle and live an abundant life. I always had drive, wanted better in life and tried to never settle for less.

I was then introduced to a new friend, and we became roommates. Life was great in the beginning. I was going out and finally enjoying my life like a typical 19-year-old. Again, however, I was looking for love in the wrong places. I got involved with a new person, one thing led to another, and I ended up pregnant again.

I was so scared and had no idea what I was going to do. I saw how hard I was struggling to raise my daughter alone working two jobs and going to school, so I decided that I was going to have an abortion. I made an appointment at the women's clinic. When I arrived, my knees were shaking, my hands were sweating, and my heart was hurting from how fast it was beating.

I went to the bathroom to provide a urine sample. I fell to my knees and started crying, started praying to God because my whole life I had lived off faith. While sitting on the floor, I heard the sound of a baby crying. I quickly got up and left the building. At that moment, hearing that child's cries, I decided to keep the baby. I knew this new relationship was not going to work but, even if I had to, I was going to do it alone.

At approximately 15 weeks pregnant, I went to find out what the sex of the baby was. While waiting for the nurse to do the ultrasound, I remembered lying on the bed and praying to God for the baby not to be a girl because I had known all I had suffered and didn't want another daughter to have to suffer because the world was so cruel, so I prayed for the baby to be a boy.

When I found out I was pregnant with my son, I was excited, but I was even more scared to have to do it alone but there was no turning back. During my pregnancy, my son's father moved away. He was not excited about the baby coming and wanted me to have the abortion. He said he was not ready to raise a child. I understood; we were just friends and roommates but I had ended up pregnant.

So, I was alone most of my pregnancy and was raising my daughter alone. I cried almost my whole pregnancy. I felt anxious, depressed, ashamed and disappointed. I didn't know if I was making the correct decision, and I was scared of the unknown. I continued to go to school but was able to find a job that allowed me to work at home, which was so much more convenient for me and my daughter. I worked at home for the remainder of my pregnancy.

My son's father had a change of heart, and we decided that we wanted to give it a try and start a real relationship. We ended up moving back in together.

REFLECTIONS: How does this chapter relate to things in your own life?

−CHAPTER 9−
I SUFFER WITH MY OWN FORMS OF DEPRESSION

After having my son, my life changed again. He was the second best thing that had ever happened to me. I was so excited but extremely nervous. My daughter was two years old, and my son was a newborn. I promised to love them forever and unconditionally no matter what happened.

After having my son, I was diagnosed with depression, anxiety and post-traumatic stress disorder (PTSD) due to all the trauma I had gone through in my life. After arriving home from the hospital with my baby boy, I got postpartum depression and would sit on the floor in his room and just cry with him. He would cry all the time and barely slept some days. I felt lost and alone.

I was the primary caretaker at home with both of the kids. I stayed home for six weeks on maternity leave from work. There were times when I knew my son was safe in the crib and I had to walk away because I would get too frustrated with his constant crying. Nothing seemed to make him happy. I sought counseling because I was scared and didn't want anything to happen to myself or the baby.

—PSALMS 127:3—

Children are a gift from the Lord; they are a reward from him.

I stayed with my son's father as we built a family and worked on our relationship. He worked full-time so he was hardly ever home. When my son turned six weeks old, I went back to work full-time and went back to school. I no longer wanted to work from home so, both of my children had to go to daycare.

Once again, school became my escape from all the pain I was still holding in my heart from my past life. I had not yet healed from it, and while I still had a long way to go for the healing process, I simply ignored my feelings and I continued to struggle emotionally after having both of my children.

I would hug them and show them affection, but it felt so awkward. I was always somewhat distanced from them and did not know how to love them because that was never taught to me. I took care of them by providing them what they needed but I knew that was still not enough. At times, I saw myself acting like my mother with her terrible attitude. It upset me to see myself slipping into that familiar behavior. I continued to seek help to better myself for my son and daughter's sake. They were the ones who needed me the most.

I then graduated from college and was able to attend my graduation. It was the best day ever for me. My mother was there with my kids, my mother's boyfriend at the time, and my son's father. I was so excited for her to be there because I wanted her to be proud of me despite her saying I would be a nobody. Many people had declared me a loss including my mother. I was the first person in my family's generation to graduate both high school and college.

Even with having two children, I never gave up on my dreams. I never made excuses or told myself I couldn't do it. Many people said I was crazy and I needed to quit. They thought that because I was a mother, I needed to spend more time with my children. I never forgot for one moment that I was a mother. I just wanted better for our life, and I wanted to live the best life I could provide them. I did not want to settle for less. I had seen growing up what happened when you settled for less. So, I wanted more, and less was not an option for me.

—PSALMS 23:4—

Even though I walk through the darkest valley, I will fear no evil, for you are with me; your rod and your staff, they comfort me.

REFLECTIONS: How does this chapter relate to things in your own life?

—CHAPTER 10—
NO GOOD DEED GOES UNPUNISHED

We had also let my partner's family move into our house because they had nowhere to go that year. I have to say that it was the worst decision I had ever made. Sometimes family can be the worst and most evil people ever. His family were so disrespectful in my home. They did not like me, and I never understood why. They were very toxic and would get me and my husband to argue.

Suffice it to say, I had to tell them to leave my home. They were so angry at me for telling them to leave, they started doing very mean things. They called child protective services on me and made up so many lies in an effort to destroy my life. They got me fired from my job from the lies they were spreading about me.

My husband did not help much with the bills. So, shortly afterwards, our electricity was shut off. There were days we had no food to eat. I had to ask for assistance at local churches and charity places. I lived paycheck to paycheck even though I worked a full-time job. So, being jobless for a few weeks created a void and a huge struggle.

I was able to find a new job, but his family continued to stalk me where I now worked and followed me around trying to create trouble for me. I didn't understand how people could be so cruel. But I never gave up. It was not optional; my son and my daughter needed me.

—LUKE 6:27-28—

But I tell you who hear me: Love your enemies, do good to those who hate you, bless those who curse you, pray for those who mistreat you."

—PHILIPPIANS 4:13—

I can do all things through Christ which strengtheneth me.

—DEUTERONOMY 31:6—

Be strong and courageous. Do not be afraid or terrified because of them, for the LORD your God goes with you; he will never leave you or forsake you."

REFLECTIONS: How does this chapter
relate to things in your own life?

−CHAPTER 11−
BIG MOVES AND CHANGES

I decided to move to Virginia because I wanted to go into the Navy. I wanted something different. I took the ASVAD exam and passed with high scores. I started working out and preparing myself physically and emotionally.

I married my son's father. We had a small intimate wedding with close family and friends. I had an aunt who lived in Virginia, and I told her I wanted to move there. She said, yes. So, we went to visit in February, and I fell in love with the place.

Before arriving, I started to apply for jobs. I had scheduled a few interviews so that when I got there, I could do the interviews while visiting. After having a job interview at a hospital, I was immediately offered the job. I told my husband we were moving. I was so excited for a change and for this move. While visiting, I got with a realtor and started looking at homes to purchase.

We returned home and started making the arrangements required to move. I began to sell everything that was in our home in Florida. We traveled with a U-Haul truck with just the basic things we needed. I was ready to start a new life and leave all the baggage behind. Within a month or so, we had moved to my aunt's house. She opened her home to me and my family.

I was full of determination and perseverance. I was never going to give up on anything. I knew this move was going to be for the best because I was going to make it happen.

My husband decided that he did not want me to go into the Navy; he had changed his mind. So, to appease him, I ended up not going and continued to work at the hospital. I would wake up every day and take the children to daycare and go to work. I worked roughly an hour and a half drive away from my aunt's house. My travel time, with dropping the children off at daycare, would take me almost two hours in the morning and two hours in the afternoon.

With my children in daycare, the hope was that my husband could find a job. We were struggling because he could not seem to find a job that he liked or that made sense. He started back up again drinking alcohol and taking sleeping pills. I knew he had somewhat of a drinking problem but I never realized how bad it had gotten. It began to become more obvious that he had a serious problem. I thought it was going to get better with the move but it didn't. Thankfully, he eventually found a job and that helped.

After a long search, I was able to purchase my first home at age 21 in Virginia. Yes, 21! I had a credit score of 545 and $6,000, which was the three percent I needed for the down payment. I qualified for an FHA Loan to purchase my house. Due to my husband's bad credit and financial situation, I purchased the home alone. This was a very happy moment and an accomplishment for myself. I knew I was headed in the right direction in providing my children a home with security and stability.

REFLECTIONS: How does this chapter relate to things in your own life?

–CHAPTER 12–
FAILURE IS NOT AN OPTION

I continued to work and my two children went to daycare, but that did not last very long. My children were always sick, and the daycare workers did not provide proper care for them. The staff didn't even know their names after being there for a few weeks, and my children were so unhappy.

I tried in-home daycare on one occasion but my daughter and son were locked in a room and forced to take a nap all alone. The daycare worker also hit my daughter for breaking a toy. My son would come home with the same diaper he had from when I had changed him before going to daycare that morning. Both of my children were always sick from the lack of sanitation from these places.

When I would pick up my children, I would cry and felt desperate because my number one job was to always make sure my children were taken care of. I was desperate. I knew I had to work and felt like I had no escape, but I was done. So, I quit my job. I then found a job where I worked nights and on the weekends so my husband could stay with the children. That did not work out very long because my husband would wait for me to get home to do the house duties and to cook for everyone. He would be drunk sleeping on the floor while the children were running around the house.

So, I quit my job again. I felt like if it was not one thing, it was always another. I could not get a break from the madness, Life started to get hard. I was living in a state with no support and hardly any family. I truly felt alone but giving up was not an option for me.

So, I decided that instead of working away from the house, I did the opposite. I decided to open my doors to other families and provide much needed quality care and education for their children. This way, I could be home to take care of my own children and offer the same care and education to other parents who needed someone who would take the job seriously and who could be trusted to take good care of their children. As time went by, my waiting list got longer and longer. Owning a school had always been my dream. So, I began to look for a building to house my growing business.

With only $10,000 to open a business, I began construction on the first location, and I opened my first childcare center. Everything and anything that could possibly go wrong, went wrong. I had to borrow money so I could stay open and pay for the remainder of the construction.

I woke up early every day and worked very hard. I stayed up late even when I was tired, and my body was exhausted and couldn't do it anymore. I still pushed myself regardless, and made it happen. I knew it was going to be a journey to make my dreams come true. It did not matter to me how long it was going to take.

I kept God in my life, and it kept me humbled. I continued to keep God first in my life and even when I didn't stick with him, he stuck with me.

Failure was not an option for me. I had to lose my fear of failure and of the unknown because failure was part of the process. You have to get it wrong to get right. On many occasions, I doubted myself but I kept pushing towards what I really wanted.

I had to put on the armor of God. I was fighting a spiritual warfare within myself. I had fears, doubts, anxiety, and insecurities. I fought with haters, liars, betrayal, and backstabbers. I even had to fight with my family and many times I lay in bed crying. I couldn't sleep because I was fighting with myself.

We never know what people go through. Having to cope with life and being me was not easy, it definitely was not for the faint of heart. It was like running a marathon that did not have a destination. When your body begins to hurt, you feel fatigued and your heart is racing, it's time to strap up your boots, face your fears of failure, and keep going.

—EPHESIANS 6:10-17—

Finally, be strong in the Lord and in his mighty power.

Put on the full armor of God, so that you can take your stand against the devil's schemes.

For our struggle is not against flesh and blood, but against the rulers, against the authorities, against the powers of this dark world and against the spiritual forces of evil in the heavenly realms.

Therefore put on the full armor of God, so that when the day of evil comes, you may be able to stand your ground, and after you have done everything, to stand.

Stand firm then, with the belt of truth buckled around your waist, with the breastplate of righteousness in place,

and with your feet fitted with the readiness that comes from the gospel of peace.

In addition to all this, take up the shield of faith, with which you can extinguish all the flaming arrows of the evil one.

Take the helmet of salvation and the sword of the Spirit, which is the word of God.

REFLECTIONS: How does this chapter
relate to things in your own life?

–CHAPTER 13–
MY HUSBAND AND MY MARRIAGE FALLS APART

While trying to manage a new business, dealing with my husband at the time, and trying to raise my children, things got hectic. This took a toll on our marriage, which lasted only a few years. I tried everything. I was committed to attending much-needed counseling but he refused.

I could no longer deal with his drinking problem and had to face the difficult fact that my husband was an alcoholic and was not willing or able to change. He would lie about his drinking, which began to severely affect our relationship and finances. We had many disagreements about his drinking problems. He would often take money from our accounts to support his habit. He would struggle to get up to go to work because he had been drinking the whole night before. This behavior triggered my previous trauma and seeing my husband drunk and falling over everywhere brought many emotions back from my childhood.

I knew my first priority was to protect my children. He would say he was not drinking but he would hide the cups and bottles of vodka in the house, hoping I would not find them. He was financially draining our household. He was always late on the bills and could not meet financial obligations. His credit score continued to drop. He would not last very long on a job due to his issues. We argued daily, and our marriage and relationship got worse and worse. He also would cheat on me with other women and lie about his indiscretions.

I would pray to God to please heal him. When I caught him taking money from my business accounts, at that very moment, I knew I was done. While sitting on the porch outside one day, he asked me if I no longer wanted to be with him and I said, "Yes, I am done. I can't take this anymore." He went back into the house, packed all his things, put them in his car, and left.

I soon discovered that he had started sleeping in my school at night and would leave in the morning before the school opened at 6:00 a.m. I went into the school one Sunday because something seemed unusual. I would go into work and see cans of beer in the bathrooms and thought, Who is doing this? I began to wonder if it was the contractors that worked in my building to do repairs. So, one day, I went to deliver supplies on a Sunday night and saw him sleeping on a sleeping mat with a 6-pack of beer. I was heartbroken to see him like this. I asked myself why couldn't he change. I knew I could not change anyone and that change had to come from them. So, I walked away, crying to see my son's father and my husband be so broken. I knew he had hit rock bottom.

He eventually found his own place and seemed to do a bit better. He would visit the children. My daughter did not know who her real father was because my ex-husband had raised her from eight months old. My ex-husband had signed all the documents when my daughter was little to adopt her after we got married. He loved her and treated her like his own child. He was not a bad person but he was just so broken. I had my hands full with the business and raising the children and I simply could not deal with his drinking, cheating and other problems.

Sadly, he ended up moving out of state and stopped seeing the children. Afterwards, I was awarded full and sole custody of the children due to his problems. It was a very hard time for both of my children. I had to put both of them in counseling to help them cope with their father abandoning them and not having any contact with him.

Even with all of this, I never allowed anyone to see what I was going through. I was very reserved and private about my personal life. I never took my issues to work or discussed them with anyone, not even friends, for fear of being judged. I was embarrassed and ashamed of what was happening in my life.

REFLECTIONS: How does this chapter relate to things in your own life?

–CHAPTER 14–
OVERCOMING FINANCIAL DIFFICULTIES

*T*he marriage had ended a year after my business opened. When my husband left, he took all the money out of the bank accounts. Because of this, my home was going into foreclosure. At the time, I had no income. I was trying to keep my business open but it was not making a profit yet. Most businesses don't turn a profit in the first couple of years.

Life was tough, but what kept me going was my perseverance and determination. I simply refused to go down without a fight. I had faith and believed in God. I prayed every day and believed God was on my side. I didn't understand why all of this was happening to me, but I just continued to keep my faith. I knew the only person that could get me through my troubles and had brought me this far in life was God.

I began to research and looked for resources that might help with my sinking finances. I worked 15 to 16 hours a day in my business so I could start to pay myself. I went into complete debt, and my credit score was awful but my tenacity eventually paid off, and I survived. The warrior in me did not allow me to give up.

I think of my journey like a pregnant woman with a baby growing in her womb. I had pains that felt like contractions and all the symptoms of a pregnancy, but I continued to push even though I had so little strength left. My body was weak but my faith was stronger. My nine months of growing my business was nearly as hard as my childhood but all those difficult things I had experienced at such an early age had prepared me for this even more than I realized. All my trials made me stronger, and I learned that I had it in me to keep going. I didn't know everything I was going through was preparing me for what I had asked God for. I also did not know the process was going to be necessary to get me where I was going.

At month nine of the business, it was like I had finally given birth. All the pain was over, but the baby began to grow. In fact, it was growing almost faster than I could handle. Every day, when I went to work, I prayed over the children and families I served daily and anointed the building with oil. I knew God had a bigger plan for me. I was just unsure what was going to happen next.

I kept pushing forward and I was determined not to have to live in my car or go back home due to my circumstances. My business took a year and a half to get off the ground, and I made it through.

While everything was happening in my life, I never allowed anyone to see the madness and stress I was going through. I cried every night and wanted to fix everything and everyone, but I knew that was not possible. And, because of what I went through in my life, I knew I wanted something different for my children. My whole life I had lived under a mask. I was scared to be judged because of all I had gone through. I wanted to free myself from the jail in my mind that I had placed myself in.

My business continued to grow after the divorce. Life was finally getting better after twenty-four years of pain. I was at a place in my life where I had complete control of every aspect of it. I was beginning to create the life I truly wanted.

I then lost my grandmother, the only person who had believed in me and who helped me. I lost the only person I could talk to and go to for advice. My grandmother was tough but she was also the only person who genuinely showed me affection and love. I loved her dearly. I didn't always agree with her, but she was really the only person who had tried to protect me regardless of the risk.

A year later, my oldest brother committed suicide. He hung himself in his jail cell on Mother's Day. When I got the call, I took the first flight to Florida to be there to support my mother who I felt needed me. This was the brother who had caused me so much pain and trauma. What can I say? I was sad in some ways, but I felt the person who had hurt me was gone, and I didn't have to worry about him hurting me or anyone else ever again. I eventually forgave him for all that he had done to me.

For many years afterwards, I tried to build a relationship with my mother, but unfortunately, the relationship was just too toxic. I have finally forgiven her for all she did to me as well, but I have learned to love her from afar. I had to learn to set boundaries for everyone in my life and not to allow anyone to mistreat me. I had to believe that I deserved to be loved and respected. After my whole life dealing with hurt and betrayal, I knew I deserved so much more and was not going to let anyone else treat me any less, even if it meant cutting ties with them.

Shortly after my divorce was final and I was finally living the life I always wanted, I paid off all of my debt and I was living the life God had promised me. I was working on myself and starting to heal my soul. My children were happy. I was happy and finally smiling. I started working on myself by eating healthy, working out, spending time with my children, and being present in my life all the time. I also started traveling and living life and all it had to offer me. I was buying my children everything they needed and wanted and taking them on vacations often, because, at this point in our life, I could afford to do what I wanted. To me there was no limit. I was finally able to give them the life I always wanted.

The average person would have said my children were spoiled, but to me I was giving them what I had always dreamed of and what I had always wanted and never had. But I always instilled in them that they needed to earn everything and work hard for what they wanted. I continued to show my son and daughter the value of what it cost me to get where we were and how hard I had to work to get there. I started to open up with my children and explain to them some of what happened to me in my childhood. I wanted them to understand that they were very fortunate to have all they did because I was not as fortunate at their age.

I continued to work and build my businesses. At this point, I had built a million-dollar company. Life was great, and I was doing so much better.

REFLECTIONS: How does this chapter relate to things in your own life?

—CHAPTER 15—
RECONNECTING WITH SOMEONE SPECIAL: TRIGGERS

One morning, I was getting ready to get on an early morning flight to go on vacation with my children when I received a message from my best friend. We had not spoken for a long time. We had known each other for about ten years. We connected while I was on vacation and got to know each other very well.

After the vacation, we talked every day and spoke for hours on end. We began to visit each other very frequently. It was like a love story. For the first time in my life, I was starting to genuinely fall in love with a person and was trying to open my heart. We went on many more vacations and started to build a deep bond with one another.

He started to spend more time with my children. They absolutely loved the time they spent with him. He always made them feel special and important. I started to feel butterflies in my stomach. This was the only adult male they had ever been around other than my ex-husband. He made me feel special, and as if I was the only woman in the world.

We lived in different states though, and love from a distance was very hard, but we continued to make it work. On one vacation we went on, we were on our way home and I started to cry uncontrollably. I didn't understand what was happening. I didn't realize I was falling in love with this man.

I had created the appearance of a strong and brave individual and never showed weakness. For my entire life, I assumed that love was for weak people. And I thought I always had to be this strong and fearless woman who didn't allow feelings to run her life. I believed that people would take my love as weakness and hurt me. Besides, both he and I had our careers, and we were completely stable. For me, there was not an option for me to move. I had to think of the businesses I had built. My whole life, the people who said they loved me always ended up hurting me.

So, on our way home from that vacation, I started to feel scared and unsafe. I wasn't sure of his intentions, and I didn't want to risk our friendship to find out. I had always lived in defense mode and would attack anyone who became too close in my space. I began to put a wall around my heart to guard my feelings. Being vulnerable was not for me; it just meant that people were going to take advantage of me. I had come too far and worked too hard to allow anyone to take advantage of me ever again.

So, I became aggressive with my feelings. I tried to end the relationship multiple times. I became mean towards him and stopped calling him and answering his calls but he tried to keep things going with me. At the time, he didn't know about my childhood issues. I hadn't shared my past in depth with him. He knew some of it, but not everything. I was embarrassed and ashamed to tell someone I cared this much for what I had been through in my life and that was why I was acting the way I was. I was even ashamed to say I was scared to get too close to him. It triggered so many emotions because of my past trauma.

The people who said they loved me would end up hurting me physically and emotionally. So, when he showed me something different, I didn't know how to react. When he would caress me, I would jump from fear. And I thought to myself that this was too good to be true. How can someone be so patient, caring and kind? I had prided myself on being this fearless woman who never showed emotions.

I also wanted to guard my children so not him or anyone could hurt them again. My children continued to talk to him because they enjoyed that he provided that safe space they wanted and needed and gave them the undivided attention they were looking for.

I continued to grow and work on my business. This very patient man continued to be in our lives even though I was trying everything to push him away. Finally, he decided he was going to move to the state I was in. Of course, I was not very happy about him being in my physical space because I only considered the worst-case scenarios but he was determined he was going to make this work while I continued to sabotage everything due to my insecurities.

The relationship was great some days, but I struggled other days because we were very different people and had different upbringings. I was a very independent woman who was not looking for someone to save her. He was very nurturing and showed lots of affection where I was the total opposite. Showing affection was not something I knew. He struggled in his own way as well.

When I made up my mind, no one was going to change it. Is that called stubbornness? Well, then yes, that was me. I am very ambitious and a visionary. I knew where I wanted to go in life and where I wanted to be. He was very passive and lived life very slowly.

I realized that I had an issue so I started seeking counseling to help me figure out the root of the problem. After a few months, I discovered I had so much built up from my past life experiences that loving someone other than my children was going to be difficult and was going to take time. I needed so much healing and needed to release all that I had been through. I was still keeping myself captive. I thought I was doing better, and while everything was going great, everything also triggered my feelings and came back triple fold when this man came into my life. I told myself, this is not great, there is so much work that needs to be done.

However, this man continued to support me even after he heard about everything I had been through in my life. He helped me continue to grow my business and supported me while I was finishing my master's degree. When we went on vacations, life was great but when we got back to real life I had to deal with the reality of my issues.

Yes, it was not easy living with me. I had created very high standards for myself and was not going to settle for anything less. He continued to be very patient knowing that it was not going to be easy. He had his own flaws, but don't we all? I just didn't know how to support someone else's flaws because I had so many of my own.

I was not ready for a relationship. I had and still have so much healing I need to do but we have continued to still be great friends and be there for each other. My children absolutely love and adore him. He has always treated them as his own. He attends most of their soccer games and gymnastic practices, and the children love him for it. I wouldn't trade the relationship they have built over the years for anything.

While he works on his flaws, I will continue to work on mine. He is truly my best friend, my confidante, and my shoulder to cry on. This relationship is a good example of how your past can affect your present if you don't deal with the big problem. Taking counseling helped connect the dots as to why I was aggressive with my emotions and feelings and all the triggers I was experiencing. You can't erase your past history but you can decide if it's going to be part of your future.

REFLECTIONS: How does this chapter
relate to things in your own life?

—CHAPTER 16—
UNEXPECTED STRUGGLES

*L*ater on, my son began to have severe behavior issues at home and at school. He was diagnosed with attention deficit and hyperactivity disorder (ADHD) and oppositional defiant disorder (ODD). My son became very angry and aggressive towards everyone. He hated everything and everyone because he started to miss his father. He started to steal from school and even stores.

I thought I had failed him completely. He would kick the walls in my home and would do things to set the house on fire unintentionally. He would say things like everyone hated him and that he wanted to kill himself. It was so hard to see my son going through this in his young life. I would pray over him, and I was just so upset and angry at myself because I was trying everything to help him, and nothing was working.

I had to put him back into counseling to help him learn to regulate his emotions and express them in appropriate ways. He was trying everything to get kicked out of school. He was just so angry. I continued to show him love and that I was there for him, but it seemed that I was the last person he wanted around him.

He was so rebellious. I would go to my room and cry, asking God to please help my son and give him what he needed and to give me the patience to help him. With my past experiences in life, I was determined I was not going to put my son on medication. But nevertheless, I had to, but I was very cautious about the medication that was given to him. We tried six or seven different medications to find one that worked best for his body. (Note to reader: When we think everything is going great, something always happens, it's just part of life. Giving up should never be an option no matter what obstacles life throws at you.)

Then the 2020 Covid pandemic happened. My life and the life of most of the people around the world changed completely. I was worried that I was going to lose everything I had worked so hard for. But, my survival instincts kicked in, and I started working even harder to make sure we were able to make ends meet. At this point, I knew I was doing what I was called to do and it was to serve children and their families.

Business began to pick up again and was doing great. We had more children than we could handle and a long waiting list. I knew that I wanted another location to serve more children. I wanted to add more space so more children could be served and have a safe place while receiving quality care and a quality education while being nurtured and properly taken care of. So, I began looking for a location. During my search, I found what I thought was the perfect building but to say the least, it was not God's plan.

I found another location in a different area, so I quickly signed the paperwork for my second location and construction began.

Right before opening, however, I had a stroke. What led to my stroke was extremely high levels of stress with no rest period that caused my blood pressure to increase for long periods of time. I was working long hours, eating out almost every day. I was not sleeping. My brain was on overload, and I could not shut it off.

It had gone on like this for months. The day I was having my stroke, I clearly did not know it was a stroke. I could have never imagined having a stroke because I was young and pretty healthy. I just thought I was overworked and stressed.

While managing my first location and opening the second location, it was very stressful. As always, I never asked for help. I thought I could do anything and everything alone. A few days prior, I had begun to feel tension and tightness in the right side of my neck and shoulder; it felt like a pinched nerve. I knew it was coming from the high levels of stress. This had been going on for months; it just kept getting worse by the day. I felt my heart racing but I thought it was normal because I was constantly on the go.

Prior to the stroke, I had taken my blood pressure, and it was double digits on the top and on the bottom, but I kept going. I also began to have severe migraines, which I had always suffered since a teenager so I thought it was just another migraine that would go away after rest and treatment.

A year prior to my stroke, I had a migraine for over 30 days with no relief. I had to go to the hospital for treatment because it was so extreme that it would cause blurry vision and extreme head pain that no medication would help relieve.

I kept working and said to myself that nothing was going to stop me, so I went to work that morning. I felt weak and was slower than normal. My right arm felt numb and my face on the right side was tingling. I finished working in the new location and drove myself to the first location. When I arrived, my arm and shoulder were in extreme pain.

At this point, I had not told anyone what was happening. One of my supervisors noticed something was wrong with me so she quickly advised me that I needed to be seen. I fussed because I was just stressed and had work to get done. She insisted and contacted the urgent care, and they advised I go straight to the hospital. She drove me and met with my significant other, and he drove me immediately to the hospital.

We first stopped to eat because I said I was hungry and immediately he noticed something wrong with my face because I was not able to swallow. He rushed me quickly to the hospital and shortly after, they had discovered I was having a stroke. I was admitted for two days and released to go home.

What can I say? I was angry, and I cried out to God and asked why me and why did this happen to me? I was doing all he had asked of me. I struggled with the basics of even having to dress myself, cook, or open doors. Writing anything was very challenging and to say the least, driving was next to impossible.

I am dominantly right-handed, so my life changed. I had to take physical therapy for six months and learn to write with my left hand in order to get some normality in my life while I recovered.

This was my wake-up call. All I knew was that I never wanted to be in this position ever again because my children needed me. I saw their faces of pity, and they were so sad to see me in this condition. I knew I was going to make a change.

I won't tell you it has been easy because it has not. I struggle every day to give myself the self-care I need to rest and regroup, but I try to put in the effort to not overwork myself. Our bodies talk to us prior to us getting sick or when something is wrong, but at times, we ignore all the signs that our bodies are giving us because we are too busy and on the go. We must take the time to take care of ourselves first to be any good for our loved ones. Life is too short, so never take for granted what is in front of you because the next day is not promised.

Then, that evening, while crying, I realized that God had prepared me with all the necessary tools for what I was going through in my life while creating me in my mother's womb.

I began to pray, "Dear God, when I start to get consumed by my worries, please help me remember that you are in control and that you've got me and made a way for me. Lord, I surrender all my worries to you and trust that you have gone ahead of me. Thank you for your love, grace, for covering me, and for your protection. In Jesus name, I pray Amen."

—PHILIPPIANS 4:6-7—

Rejoice in the Lord always. I will say it again: Rejoice! Do not be anxious about anything, but in everything, by prayer and petition, with thanksgiving, present your requests to God. And the peace of God, which transcends all understanding, will guard your hearts and your minds in Christ Jesus.

Shortly after my stroke, I graduated with my master's degree in Clinical Psychology. This was such a huge accompaniment for me. Even with the crazy life I had lived, I never gave up on school or my dreams. I went to graduation and was so happy to finally walk the stage and see where I finally was in my life.

—PROVERBS 24:33-34—

He who loves to sleep and the folding of hands, poverty will set upon you like a thief in the night.

REFLECTIONS: How does this chapter relate to things in your own life?

–CHAPTER 17–
BIG BUILDING, BIG TRAUMA, BIG WORK

Many people think once you're at the top, the challenges stop, which unfortunately that is not the truth.

I began to have my troubles again with my son. The challenges started after returning to school. Due to the pandemic, he had to reacclimate after being home for almost a year doing virtual learning. His counseling had to stop during the pandemic as well because everything went virtual, which didn't work for him.

He was put on a new medication that gave him depressive and suicidal side effects. He would put a hoodie over his head and only wanted to wear dark clothing and always wanted to be alone.

I quickly started to look for counselors and get him into any program I could find that might help him. I eventually found an in-home counseling program where the counselor came to our house four days a week. I knew giving up on my son was not an option.

Many times he said to me that he hated me and that I was ruining his life. He was angry because he missed his father but his father would refuse to call him. It took a lot of work but now I am happy to say that things have begun to be somewhat better for my son. It is still a struggle some days but I wouldn't have it any other way.

A year later, I was contacted by the owner of that first building I had fallen in love with, even though at the time, it was not meant to be. I continued to drive by the building and prayed over that building every day. I would dream about this place and could see me in it. I knew and had faith that the building was going to be mine.

So, a meeting was set up by the realtor to see the property and do a walk-through. The building had been closed for two years. It was in complete disarray and destroyed. When I walked in the building, there were mice everywhere. At that very moment, all the triggers I thought were gone came back. I started screaming from panic.

The realtor was so scared and my significant other screamed for me to walk out the room but my feet felt stuck to the floor. I froze and couldn't move. I just continued to scream. I remembered all I had gone through as a child and all the memories had come back from when that lady used to throw the mice in the room, and I was petrified.

Every emotion and feeling came back. How embarrassing it was to have to explain this to someone. I was always embarrassed of my life and I was ashamed of everything.

For a few weeks, I pondered if I really wanted this location. I started to have bad dreams and night terrors that the mice were everywhere in my home and all in my room. It was so traumatizing to me but I had to face my fears because I still saw the potential of the building.

I was not going to give up. So, the owner decided to sell me the building and I purchased it. At that moment, I knew it was God, but he needed to prepare me for what was going to come. I knew what my plan was with the building so, we started to clean the entire building. Yes, I screamed and cried and was scared every time I walked in the place where we had to kill over 200 mice and had also placed over 300 traps because the place was completely infested.

After most of the cleanout was done, we hired an exterminator to help with the remainder. We redid the outside and gave the building a new face. What can I say? I am in complete awe with this place. I know God's plan is big with this building.

I then opened a nonprofit. This building is going to house low income and underserved families and provide a training location for mothers that need a second chance and help with a GED or high school or even a career center. I am currently in the search of a home for mothers and children in domestic violence situations that need a place to restart their life. And while going back to school or working, they can bring their children to the center to have safe care and quality education.

At this point in my life, I have opened multiple locations and own multiple seven figure companies and have invested in multifamily properties. I know many people may think, "I can't do what she did or be where she's at." Yes, you can, this is possible for anyone. It is never too late to start living your dreams. It does not matter the age or where you came from or where you are in your life. When people look at me, they say, "Wow, she has it all put together," not knowing what I had to go through to get where I am today. It was not an easy journey.

This question is for the reader: if you had to go through what I went through growing up, would you have chosen that route?

I still suffer from PTSD, anxiety, depression, and panic attacks. In my daily life, there may be things that can trigger me, but I have learned to constantly push through them. Many of you may ask what are my triggers: love, affection, stability, and police are triggers and many more.

Many of you may ask why police? Because every time we had police come to our home when I was a child, someone was getting hurt or arrested. It never seemed like they were there to help and things always escalated for the worst after their visit.

On one occasion, I was driving, and I looked out the rearview mirror of my car and saw the blue lights flashing. I instantly started to have a panic attack, my hands got sweaty, and my heart started racing, I felt the tightness in my chest, and I felt like I couldn't breathe and was gasping for air.

I quickly pulled over, thinking I was going to be stopped. It was just a sign for the officer to pass me. But, how could I have explained this if I was really being pulled over that I was scared of them and was not sure what was next. I remember my brothers getting thrown on the floor and being tazed because they were talking loudly trying to explain themselves while things escalated and the police felt intimidated, so they reacted not knowing the situation. I saw people going to jail for some things they really didn't do but because of the lies of others.

And unfortunately, the law does not have eyes so you are usually guilty until proven innocent. How scary is that? I will never say I don't believe in the law. I know the law is there to maintain order, establish standards, resolve disputes, and protect. My life truly was not easy growing up. And even as an adult I still fear the unknown.

Even with all these problems I deal with daily, they do not control me and do not dictate who I am. The problems that I still have are because of my past trauma that I have learned to overcome every single day. Every day is a struggle, but giving up is not an option. I will never forget where I came from but I never want to have to go back.

Fighting my way through and surviving has always been the way for me. When I have my mind set on a task, I become laser focused and can't stop until the project is complete. This has been an advantage for me and a disadvantage. Many would ask why it was a disadvantage and that is because unfortunately I don't know how to stop and will overwork myself until it's finished regardless of the damage I may cause myself.

What got me here was investing in myself, giving myself the self-care I needed and loving myself. I would never see the person others saw in me. Because when I saw myself in the mirror, I had a mask on, and I only took it off when I was alone.

For years, I had been searching for help, and I finally started talking to the right people. I started counseling again for myself. I struggled for so long and never knew I had the key to set free the little girl in me crying for help. My whole life I had lived with shackles that held me down because of my childhood and the mistakes of others. I finally set myself free.

REFLECTIONS: How does this chapter relate to things in your own life?

CHAPTER 18

A NOTE ON PERMISSION

Give yourself permission to love yourself enough that you can set yourself free. Asking for help is not a weakness, it's actually a strength. Give yourself grace when needed. We are humans, and humans make mistakes. I am the first to say I am the most imperfect person. I have made a million mistakes, but I have learned lessons from them all. God loves me and you with all our imperfections and flaws and that is all that matters.

I am extremely hard on myself and very critical in all I do because my entire life I was scared for people to judge me. But people are going to judge you regardless if you're doing good or bad, so who cares? The people who point fingers and judge are unhappy with themselves so they must judge others to make themselves feel satisfied.

Set boundaries and don't allow anyone in who is going to hurt you, including family. It is okay to set boundaries. When I learned to set boundaries, my whole life changed for the better. I will not allow someone to come into my space who is going to hurt me or my children in any kind of way. I have lost many friends and family members, and I am okay with that because they could not respect my boundaries.

Enjoy and love the people who enjoy being around you. I promised myself I would never force myself to be in someone's life who doesn't want me or that I must change (them or me) to be accepted. I was that person who would belittle myself to make others feel comfortable. I would get up from my seat to allow others to sit at the table. For years, I asked myself why. There was no reason, but I was broken and could not accept who I was and what I was becoming. I had no self-esteem. I was ashamed of who I was.

Give yourself permission to love yourself and don't be ashamed of who you are because greater is coming and you must be ready. We must let go of the past and get out of the dark space that we have placed ourselves in because we will end up closing doors that were meant to be open. Many blessings will come but because of our ignorance, we will walk right by them. We all have great potential in us, so we must put plans in place and execute them.

What has also served me is that I am an implementer. What does it matter if you have all the knowledge but do not implement anything? Life is about execution. We must be ready to face our fears and be ready to take chances. Nothing good comes easily. We must work hard for what we want and get uncomfortable.

At times, we are so comfortable that we are not willing to do the work to move to the next level in our life. Comfort is not always good. I will say once you have taken the next steps to elevate in your life, being at the top is also very lonely. The conversations with the people you use to have are no longer going to be the same, and some people will judge you because you are growing. Your life may look different in a good way, and they may think you are changing.

—JAMES 4:1-10 (NKJV)—

Where do war and fights come from among you? Do they not come from your desires for pleasure that war in your members?

You lust and do not have. You murder and covet and cannot obtain. You fight and war. Yet you do not have because you do not ask.

You ask and do not receive, because you ask amiss, that you may spend it on your pleasures.

Adulterers and adulteresses! Do you not know that friendship with the world is enmity with God? Whoever therefore wants to be a friend of the world makes himself an enemy of God.

Or do you think that the Scripture says in vain, "The Spirit who dwells in us yearns jealously"?

But He gives more grace. Therefore, He says: "God resists the proud, But gives grace to the humble."

Humility Cures Worldliness

Therefore submit to God. Resist the devil and he will flee from you.

Draw near to God and He will draw near to you. Cleanse your hands, you sinners; and purify your hearts, you double-minded.

Lament and mourn and weep! Let your laughter be turned to mourning and your joy to gloom.

Humble yourselves in the sight of the Lord, and He will lift you up.

—HABAKKUK 2:2-3 KING JAMES VERSION (KJV)—

And the LORD answered me, and said, Write the vision, and make it plain upon tables, that he may run that readeth it. For the vision is yet for an appointed time, but at the end it shall speak, and not lie: though it tarry, wait for it; because it will surely come, it will not tarry.

The moral of these verses is that we don't have what we want because we have not asked God for what we desire. He will provide all we ask for. But we must with a heart of thanksgiving and be grateful and humbled.

REFLECTIONS: How does this chapter relate to things in your own life?

−CHAPTER 19−
TRANSPARENCY IS KEY

After many years of pondering, I was finally able to tell my daughter the truth about who her biological father was. I didn't go in depth about all that he did to me. I didn't want her to have a bad impression of him. If she is ever to meet him, I would want her to see him for who he is and form her own opinion about him. As of today, she does not want to find him or know anything about him.

She cried and didn't talk to me for a few days when I told her the truth about her life, but I gave her the space she needed. I told her that I would be there if she needed me, and I would tell her anything she wanted to know.

Yes, many people would judge my decision to wait so long to tell her. I didn't know how to tell her about him or what to do. I didn't want to ruin her childhood or for her to change because she has always had a normal childhood and is an extremely happy child, and it just never seemed like the right time. I knew when it was time, and I felt ready. My relationship with my daughter is stronger than ever. She is my best friend and my shoulder to cry on. I will always be there for her no matter what.

I have been asked by many people what my addiction is and to be honest, my addiction is work. I can work all day and work all night.

For years, I couldn't understand why I was so addicted to working until one day I realized I was running away from myself. I didn't want to have to think or deal with my emotions. Working was my distraction and escape from all that had happened and was happening in my life. If you recall in the beginning of my story, I told you that as a child my escape place was school. We try to run away from everything to avoid having to face the reality, and avoidance just makes it worse. We must face our fears.

Who would have thought this girl, a Hispanic Latina woman of color who came from Camden, New Jersey, a tough town, with an addict father, a bipolar mother, and who lived through domestic violence relationships and was a lost and broken teen mom is now a successful business woman?

Many people make it seem like it's so easy to become a millionaire. It's not easy, and it takes hard work, sacrifice, dedication, and perseverance. Be ready to make those difficult and challenging decisions.

One thing to remember is don't tell everyone your dreams or desires because you may end up telling the wrong person who could steer you away from what could have been a breakthrough in your life. You will continue to get the same results if you continue along the same path. Change must happen if you want to see a difference.

When something big was coming, my heart would start racing, my knees started to buckle, and all the worst-case scenarios would come to mind. Fear was my real enemy. But I had to face my fears and not be scared of failure.

Have you ever heard the phrase, I should have, would have, could have? They all mean I didn't try because of my fear of the unknown. But I am here to tell you it's never too late. Always remember that no matter what you have done in life, you have the right to be forgiven. I learned that living life to the fullest was hard for me because I was so scared.

We are all willing to sacrifice some things but when things get hard, we want to quit or be the first person to drown your dreams, so you give up. That is the time to keep pushing harder. Harder to me is when I feel weak and weary but I keep pushing even when I don't have any strength.

I would not be where I am today if I had quit every time things got hard because believe me, it got worse and worse. The more I followed my calling, the worse the battles and fights got. My health and my family were attacked many times.

The more God gives us, the more he requires of us. I knew the enemy wanted to destroy the plan God had for me. You must put on your blinders so you can focus your eyes strongly on what is in front of you and know that it is okay to fail. Just get back up as quickly as you can and try again. Life will knock you down a million times, but you must be willing to get up a million and one times to see your success and progress.

My heart has always been to help people and make an impact on others. My heart goes to women and children because I am a woman and a mother and I struggled, but I was able to overcome everything that I had been through in my life and was able to not only survive but thrive and become very successful despite all of my challenges. My hope now is to be able to help someone in need and make a difference with my story. And my plan is to help others accomplish not only what I have been able to create but to do more.

Fun fact about me: I am extremely shy, and I hate public speaking but I hope to overcome this one day. This is the first time I have told my story. My hope is that my story impacts the lives of others and to show you that we do not have to be the product of our environment. I am living proof that the change comes within us. I hope this gives you the courage to write your story because we all have a story to tell.

—PSALMS 34:18—

The LORD is close to the brokenhearted and saves those who are crushed in spirit.

LETTERS FROM MY HEART:

In the next few pages, I have written a few letters to some special people in my life.

A LETTER TO MY BEAUTIFUL DAUGHTER.

As I write this letter, I am crying my eyes out because I am just so overwhelmingly grateful and thankful for your life. I thank God every day for putting you in my life. God knew when he created you that I would need you, and he gave you to me.

You are my exact twin, every feature you have is just like me. When I look at you, I see myself as a child. It's like looking in the mirror. I live my childhood with you.

I know I have not been the most perfect mom. I have made many mistakes and had my moments of being difficult to you. I am sorry for being so hard. I love you unconditionally. You were my first love. You taught me everything I need to know.

You were my first in everything. When I found out I was having you, I was so excited but scared even when I didn't know what you were. I had already fallen in love. You have been my shoulder to cry on and have shown me how to be the best mom I could be.

It was like having a baby doll. I took you everywhere, and I promised myself I would protect you with everything in me, and never allow anyone to harm you. We went through so much in your young life but I knew I was going to give you the life I never had.

I never thought I could learn to love someone so much. You are growing so fast right in front of me. Time is flying, and I hope I was able to teach you to be as strong of a warrior as me.

You are my angel, and I would never change anything about you. You're the most selfless and the most caring person I have ever seen. Your heart is so big. Your love to take care of everyone is amazing. You have a passion for gymnastics and soccer. I know you are going to go far in life and become someone big.

You have been my rock since day one. I know I have been hard on you because I want you to grow up and be an amazing young woman and never settle for less in life. The sky is the limit, and you are unstoppable. My one and only daughter, I love you with my entire life. No matter what happens in life, I will love you unconditionally, and you can always know I will have your back.

A LETTER TO MY SON.

You are truly my last true love, and you were my second true love. What can I say son, you are so perfect in every way. I loved you before you were even born. My attachment with you is unique. You taught me true patience and love.

I didn't know a mother is a son's first true love and that a son is a mother's last true love. Watching you grow has been priceless.

I was going so fast before I had you that I had learn to slow down and enjoy the moment. You were just a perfect angel sent to me. Your personality is so silly, but I wouldn't trade it for any other way. I have cried because learning to be your mother has not been easy for me. I struggled in every way. You showed me the love I was missing my entire life.

I pray to God daily over your life that he may guide you and provide you all that you need. You are my best friend, and you know the exact moment I need a hug and some love, and you give it to me.

Son, you absolutely drive me crazy. Sometimes your whining and crying over everything makes me just a little crazy but I would not trade that either. Your personality is what I needed. To say the least, we have the same personality, and we tend to drive each other a little crazy sometimes. I will love you forever. You hold my heart in your hands. I will forever protect you and love you unconditionally.

LETTER TO MY MOTHER.

Thank you for bringing me into this world. I know life may not have been easy but I am beyond grateful because without my life experiences, I would not be where God wanted me to be today in life. I just wanted to say I truly forgive you for everything you have done and all I had to go through in life.

I thank you because you gave birth to me. I may not have the relationship I wanted with you, but I still love you. Having a relationship with you has had to be from afar. But only God knew why and knows his plan. My hope is that one day we can have the mother and daughter relationship I always wanted and needed. If not, it's okay. I have finally been able to forgive myself and set myself free from the captivity I had put myself in my early life.

I am finally proud of the person I have become and the mother I have taught myself to be. Hopefully, one day, you can forgive yourself as well and finally set yourself free. I know your life was not easy, but God is the only person who can heal you in its entirety. I pray he does for you like he did for me.

Thank you, again, for everything.

—EPHESIANS 4:32:—

Be kind and compassionate to one another, forgiving each other, just as in Christ God has forgiven you.

A LETTER TO MY HUSBAND.

Dear husband, a life with me won't be easy. My past trauma has taught me to guard my heart. I have created a metal wall protecting my heart. I talk back, and I stand up for myself. My feelings are easily hurt. I overthink and over process everything. I often believe the worst-case scenario of what can or cannot happen.

I will need you to be very straightforward and honest with me because people in my past have proven to be deceitful and untrustworthy. I will need constant assurance of your love through words and, most importantly, proven through your actions.

I am still learning how to love myself and to see myself the way God sees me. I fight the voices in my head daily that tell me I'm not enough. I also fight anxiety and depression at times. Some days, I fight just to get out of bed because my body and mind feel weak. But, because I am a fighter and a warrior, I will fight for your love and for your heart. I promise to put

God first in our relationship. I promise to push you out of your comfort zone.

A LETTER FOR WOMEN.

I pray that my story will impact your life for the greater good and show you that life has so much more to offer and that with perseverance and determination, you can accomplish anything you put your mind to.

Always put God first in everything you do. He will provide and meet every need you may have. He will also give you what your heart may desire. You must believe that a major breakthrough in your life is about to happen. Be ready so you don't have to get ready.

The more God gives you, the more he will require of you. But you will be so blessed and see the glory that your eyes had never seen before. He will take you places that you only dream of but you must go back to the drawing board and start praying and believing his word and do as he requires and make the necessary changes needed. He will guide and protect you.

Always remember that we can change our destiny and have the power to change the environment around us. Learn to love yourself first. Take care of yourself. God is about to promote you. Stop allowing the enemy to tell you that everything you want and need is too far or you can't have it. You have the authority to receive, decree and declare over your life. You have no idea how fast God is about to answer your prayers. The power of prayer changes everything.

As women, we tend to do for everyone but forget about ourselves. I was like a flower if I was not treated with care and love. My petals began to fall, and if people were not careful, I would poke them with my thorns. The way I bloomed was with the right amount of love and care.

We have to surround ourselves with the people who truly love and care for us. Unfortunately, we all have those toxic people in our life that try to bring us down, but we have to learn to put boundaries in place to protect our wellbeing.

I want you to know that you never have to settle for less. You are the most perfect and amazing person just the way you are. We all have our troubles and are imperfect in our own ways. But God loves you even with all of your flaws. You are stronger than you think. We don't deserve for someone to mistreat us, ever. We have to love ourself enough to not put up with someone mistreating us. We deserve to be loved and respected.

—DEUTERONOMY 31:8—

The Lord himself goes before you and will be with you; he will never leave you nor forsake you.

—JOHN 15:16—

Ye have not chosen me, but I have chosen you, and ordained you, that ye should go and bring forth fruit, and [that] your fruit should remain, that whatsoever ye shall ask of the Father in my name, he may give it you.

—JOHN 14:6—

Jesus said to him, "I am the way and the truth and the life. No one comes to the Father except through me.

—PROVERBS 3:5-6—

Trust in the Lord with all your heart and lean not on your own understanding; in all your ways submit to him and he will make your paths straight.

—HEBREW 13:6—

So that we may boldly say, The Lord is my helper, and I will not fear what man shall do unto me.

REFLECTIONS: How does this chapter
relate to things in your own life?

CHAPTER 20:
LIVING YOUR BEST LIFE

*M*y purpose in writing my memoir, *Living Under the Mask*, was to delve deep into the transformative concept of living one's best life. Drawing from my own personal experiences, triumphs, and challenges, my hope is that this book will impart invaluable wisdom and actionable insights to guide readers on their own journey towards a fulfilling and purposeful existence. I want to underscore the significance of personal growth and continual self-improvement. I encourage you to step outside your comfort zone, embrace change, and pursue your dreams and aspirations with unwavering determination. I have shared anecdotes from my own life where I took risks, confronted fears, and stretched my boundaries, ultimately leading to significant personal and professional growth. By sharing these experiences, I hope that I have inspired you to recognize your own potential and strive for excellence in all areas of life.

I can't emphasize enough the importance of self-care and prioritizing one's well-being and the need for balance in life, including the importance of physical, mental, and emotional health. I strongly encourage you to make self-care a non-negotiable part of your daily routine, whether it be through exercise, meditation, journaling, or engaging in hobbies and activities that bring you joy and relaxation. Incorporate self-care into those busy schedules. Remember that taking care of oneself is not selfish but rather is necessary for overall happiness and fulfillment.

The power of mindset plays a huge role in shaping one's reality. Positive thinking can truly transform lives. Cultivate a positive mindset by practicing gratitude, reframing negative thoughts, and surrounding yourself with positive influences. I had to work hard in my life to shift my mindset allowing me to overcome obstacles, find solutions, and ultimately create the life I desired. By utilizing the transformative power of mindset, you can take control of your thoughts and beliefs, and in turn, shape your own realities.

Most importantly, make authentic connections and relationships. Surround yourself with supportive and uplifting individuals who align with your values and aspirations. I have spent much of my adult life cultivating meaningful relationships which have had positive impact on my personal and professional growth. Building and nurturing healthy connections, as well as recognizing and letting go of toxic relationships that hinder personal growth will greatly impact your life. I encourage you to invest time and energy in fostering authentic connections, as they can serve as a source of inspiration, guidance, and support on the journey to living one's best life. Lastly, I want to remind you of the significance of purpose and finding meaning in your life. Reflect on your passions, values, and unique talents, and align your actions and goals with your authentic self.

I have shared with you my own journey of discovering my purpose and how it has driven me to make meaningful contributions and create a life of fulfillment. I hope learning about my journey will help you uncover your own purpose so you will live a life aligned with your deepest desires; a life of fulfillment, purpose, and joy.

EPILOGUE

I have learned a lot, lived a lot, and accomplished a lot, but there is so much more I want to do and that needs to be done. In the next few years, my goal is to become a motivational speaker around the world. My hope is to reach more people who need encouragement and inspiration to reach their goals.

I plan to open more childcare centers and be able to help more children get a good foundational education. My next steps are to open up a home, the first of several I hope, where women dealing with domestic violence situations can live safely and get counseling and assistance. I have a degree in clinical psychology and know that I can give them some of the help they need, the resources to better their situation, schooling for their children, and the ability for them to go back to school or back to work. These women need a new foundation and a fresh start. I will likely stay in my home state and build these programs there where I can be hands on and work at an intimate level with these women and their children.

I hope that my future holds retirement by my early 50's while still making a difference in the lives of women and children I serve. I pray to be able to reap what I sowed, get to travel and spend time with kids, and maybe by then, grandkids and live my life abundantly.

After reading this book, I want you to know, dear reader, to never allow your environment to dictate where you want to go. I want you to be your own inspiration, your own cheerleader. Believe in and love yourself enough because people may not always be there for you and even if you have no one in your court, you can still conquer anything. The sky is the limit. Trust me, you can do anything you want if you have faith in yourself and put in the work. I am living proof of that!

ACKNOWLEDGMENTS

I first want to thank God, my family, my children, and my friends for supporting me in this journey.

Samantha Zayas is an accomplished individual who has made significant contributions in the field of early childhood education. She holds a bachelor's degree from the University of Central Florida and a master's degree in clinical psychology from the University of North Florida. As the CEO/owner of multi-site childcare centers, her primary goal is to provide high-quality education and a diverse environment for children, with a focus on early literacy. She aims to set a new standard in the industry and change the perception of what constitutes high-quality education and care for families in the community.

Samantha's motivation stems from her observations of children being provided with minimal education and a low-quality environment. She witnessed many children being promoted to the next level without basic reading and writing skills, which led her to establish childcare centers that prioritize the educational needs of children. She was disheartened by the lack of resources and funding in many programs, which hindered their ability to provide quality care and education.

In addition to her work in early childhood education, Samantha has also ventured into the real estate industry, investing in multi-family properties and owns multiple commercial real estate properties to diversify her portfolio. Her passion lies in making a positive impact on low-income communities and inspiring other women to achieve their dreams. Samantha is a dedicated mother of two young children, and they have further fueled her ambition to create change and provide a safe place for children and families.

During her free time, Samantha enjoys reading, spending quality time with her family, and exploring new places through travel.

www.ingramcontent.com/pod-product-compliance
Lightning Source LLC
Chambersburg PA
CBHW060237030426
42335CB00014B/1507